DO YOU REALLY WANT TO MEET
A MONKEY?

WRITTEN BY CARI MEISTER   ILLUSTRATED BY DANIELE FABBRI

Amicus Illustrated is published by Amicus
P.O. Box 1329, Mankato, MN 56002
www.amicuspublishing.us

Library of Congress Cataloging-in-Publication Data
Meister, Cari, author.
 Do you really want to meet a monkey? /
Cari Meister ; illustrated by Daniele Fabbri.
   pages cm. — (Do you really want to meet?)
 Summary: "A child goes on a rain forest adventure
and meets several different species of monkeys"—
Provided by publisher.
 Audience: Grade K to 3.
 Includes bibliographical references and index.
 ISBN 978-1-60753-456-3 (library binding : alk.
paper) — ISBN 978-1-60753-671-0 (ebook)
 1. Monkeys—Juvenile literature. 2. Rain forests—Ju-
venile literature. I. Fabbri, Daniele, 1978- ill. II. Title.
 QL737.P925M45 2015
 599.8—dc23   2013034706

Editor: Rebecca Glaser
Designer: Kathleen Petelinsek

Printed in the United States of America at
Corporate Graphics in North Mankato, Minnesota.
10 9 8 7 6 5 4 3 2 1

ABOUT THE AUTHOR

Cari Meister is the author of more than 120 books for children, including the *Tiny* series and *My Pony Jack*. She lives in Evergreen, CO and Minnetrista, MN with her husband, John, their four sons, one dog, one horse, and 4 hamsters. You can visit her online at www.carimeister.com.

ABOUT THE ILLUSTRATOR

Daniele Fabbri was born in Ravenna, Italy, in 1978. He graduated from Istituto Europeo di Design in Milan, Italy, and started his career as a cartoon animator, storyboarder, and background designer for animated series. He has worked as a freelance illustrator since 2003, collaborating with international publishers and advertising agencies.

So you say you want to meet a monkey. Not in the zoo, but face-to-face in the rainforest. But do you *really* want to meet a monkey?

Better pack your rain gear. Rainforests can be
very, very wet. At some times of the year, it rains
for days and days and days without stopping.

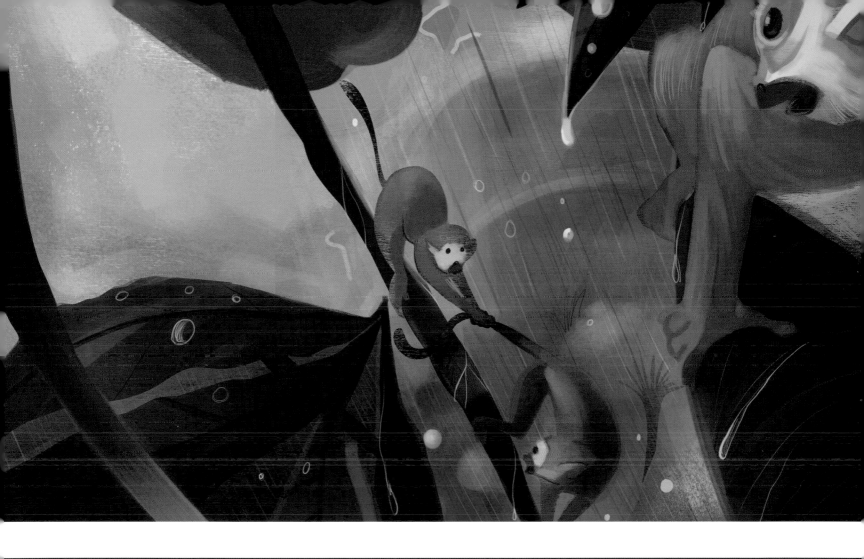

But that doesn't bother the monkeys.
Not one bit.

Keep your eyes peeled. Monkeys can be hard to find. Here's a hint. Look up. Most monkeys spend the whole day in the trees. They sleep there, too, hanging on with their tails.

Do you hear the branches shaking? Monkeys shake branches when danger is near. It's a warning signal to their friends. What's the danger? Should you run?

No. To these squirrel monkeys, YOU are the danger. After all, you are almost four times their size.

Monkeys are great tree swingers. They can move away in a hurry. You'll have to keep looking if you want to meet a monkey.

That's the sound of howler monkeys—the loudest land animals on Earth. Their calls can be heard miles away.

Male howlers have large throats and special vocal chambers that make their calls extra loud. Do you still *really* want to meet a monkey face-to-face?

Look at their big mouths! Don't worry. They won't eat you. Howler monkeys eat leaves and fruit. But sometimes they get annoyed with intruders. Guess what they do then?

Attack! Howler monkeys throw twigs and fruit at animals and people when they want them to leave. Sometimes they urinate from the trees, to really make their point.

Maybe it's time to meet some other kinds of monkeys. Ever been on a sky tram?

A sky tram is a fantastic way to see the rainforest. It's one way to get a "monkey's eye" view. You can see heaps of things from up here: tree frogs and toucans and parrots and . . .

. . . monkeys! There's a troop of spider
monkeys. But what are they doing?

They're picking bugs off each other and eating them! How appetizing. Are you hungry? Maybe a monkey will share with you. Or maybe you should stop and get a snack.

Whew! No bugs on this menu. Just a nice, refreshing
guanábana smoothie and some yucca fries. Wait!
What happened to your fries?

A little thief! Capuchin monkeys are curious
and brave. They love when tourists come to
visit. It's nice to meet you, monkey!

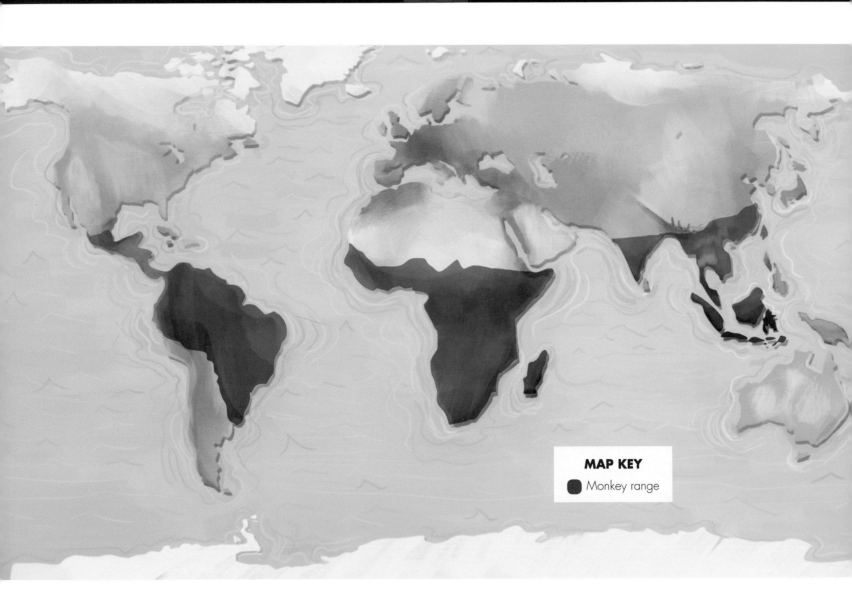

MAP KEY
● Monkey range

GLOSSARY

guanábana A large, dark green pulpy fruit, sometimes called soursop. It tastes sweet.

sky tram A passenger cart suspended from a cable.

toucan A bright-colored, fruit-eating bird with a large bill.

tourists People who travel for fun, sometimes to go on sightseeing trips.

troop A group of monkeys.

vocal chambers Special, large throat parts in howler monkeys.

yucca A cassava plant; people eat the roots of this plant like a sweet potato.

READ MORE

Bodden, Valerie. **Monkeys**. Amazing Animals. Mankato, Minn.: Creative Education, 2011.

Owen, Ruth. **Mischievous Monkeys**. New York: Windmill Books, 2012.

Sayre, April Pulley. **Meet the Howlers!** Watertown, Mass.: Charlesbridge, 2010.

Schreiber, Anne. **Monkeys**. Washington, D.C.: National Geographic, 2013.

WEBSITES

Black-Faced Spider Monkey
http://kids.mongabay.com/animal-profiles/black-faced-spider-monkey.html
See pictures and read facts about this monkey with long arms and legs.

Capuchin Monkey | San Diego Zoo—Kids
http://kids.sandiegozoo.org/animals/mammals/capuchin-monkey
Read about Capuchin monkeys, see photos, and learn about other rainforest animals too.

Howler Monkey Facts and Pictures—National Geographic Kids
http://kids.nationalgeographic.com/kids/animals/creaturefeature/howler-monkey/
Watch a video of howler monkeys in the wild.

Monkey | San Diego Zoo Animals
http://animals.sandiegozoo.org/animals/monkey
See videos and photos of monkeys at the San Diego Zoo, and learn about the many different species of monkeys and monkey behavior.

Every effort has been made to ensure that these websites are appropriate for children. However, because of the nature of the Internet, it is impossible to guarantee that these sites will remain active indefinitely or that their contents will not be altered.